The Rabbit Who Overcame Fear

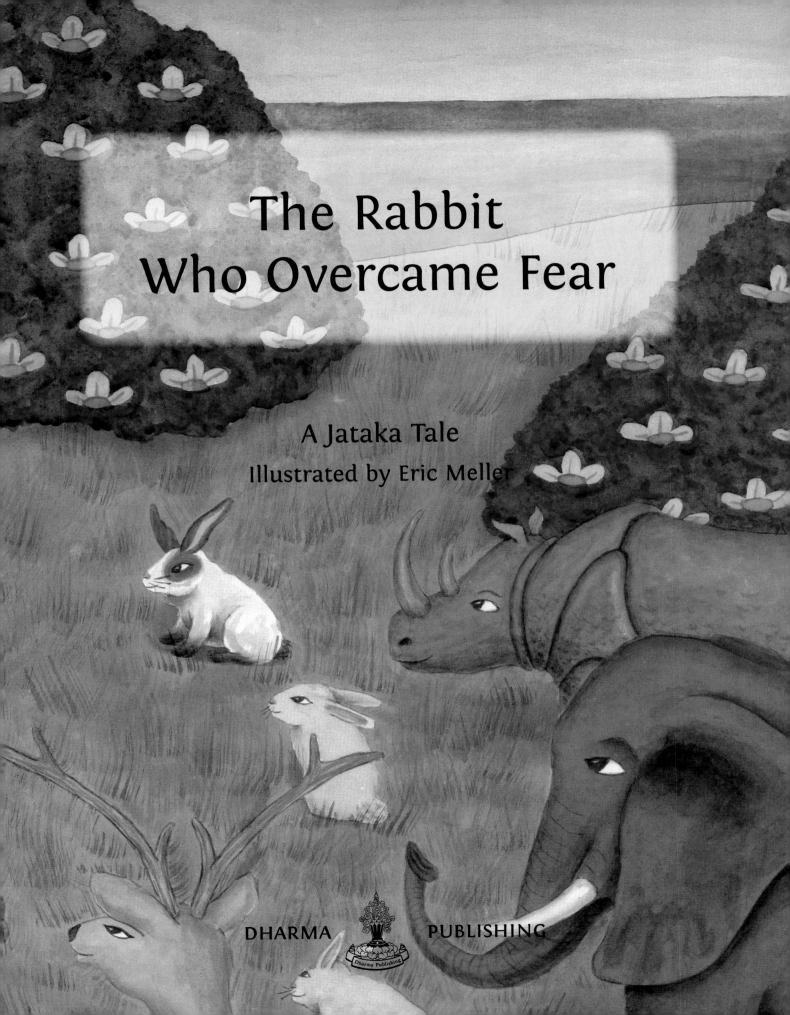

The Rabbit
Who Overcame Fear

A Jataka Tale

Illustrated by Eric Meller

DHARMA PUBLISHING

First published 1991

Second edition 2009, augmented with guidance
for parents and teachers

Printed on acid-free paper
Printed in the United States of America by Dharma Press
35788 Hauser Bridge Road, Cazadero, California 95421

9   8   7   6   5   4   3   2

Library of Congress Cataloging-in-Publication Data

The Rabbit Who Overcame Fear/illustrated by Eric Meller

(Jataka Tales Series)
Summary: A young rabbit's fear that the earth is breaking up spreads to the
other animals, until a wise lion teaches them all to investigate their fears before
jumping to hasty conclusions.

1. Jataka stories, English. [1. Jataka stories]
I. Meller, Eric, ill. II. Series
BQ1462.E5C66 1991   294.3'823-dc20   90-48400

ISBN 978-0-89800-492-2

Dedicated to children everywhere

Long ago, in the far-off land of India, a little white rabbit lived in the woods near the ocean. One sunny day he was napping under a mango tree, enchanted by the smell of ripe fruit. Nearby, his friends played in the bushes and a deer nibbled grass. The world was peaceful.

Suddenly the little white rabbit was startled awake by a loud "thud." The ground beneath him was shaking. Panicked, he jumped up and thought, "The earth must be breaking apart!" He began to run for his life.

"Why are you running?" his rabbit friends called after him. The little white rabbit turned around and cried: "The earth is breaking apart!" Terrified, the other rabbits started running too.

More and more rabbits stopped what they were doing and joined in the flight. Soon, hundreds of rabbits, eyes darting, ears twitching in fear, were scampering after the little white rabbit.

A deer saw the rabbits charging through the forest and asked, "What is the matter? Is there a fire?"

"Worse! Much worse! The earth is breaking apart!"

"Then we must tell the other animals!"

The deer told the buffalo. The buffalo told the wild ox. The wild ox told the tiger. The tiger told the elephant. The elephant told the rhinoceros. Soon, hundreds of animals were stampeding behind the little white rabbit, and their cry, "The earth is breaking apart!" rang from one end of the forest to the other.

A lion heard the thunder of hooves and ran to see what was happening. When he saw the host of animals rushing towards a cliff, the lion thought, "If I do not stop them, they will charge off the edge of the cliff and fall into the ocean."

With a burst of speed the Great Being leapt to the front of the panicked animals and stood between them and the edge. "Stop!" he roared. "Whatever are you running away from?"

"The earth is breaking apart!" all the animals said, each in his and her own way.

"Now, who saw the earth breaking apart?" asked the lion.

"The elephant saw it," snorted the rhinoceros.

"The tiger saw it," trumpeted the elephant.

"The wild ox saw it," growled the tiger.

"The buffalo saw it," bellowed the wild ox.

"The deer saw it," rumbled the buffalo.

"The little white rabbit saw it," whispered the deer.

At last the little white rabbit spoke up and said softly,
"I heard it. I heard the earth breaking apart."
"Where were you when it happened?" asked the lion.
"I was sleeping under a mango tree. Suddenly the ground
shook beneath me and I heard the most awful 'thud'."
The lion said, "Come, little rabbit, hop on my back
and together we will investigate what happened. The rest
of you stay here until we return."

With the rabbit on his back, the lion bounded through the forest until they arrived at the mango tree where the little white rabbit had been napping. "Let me down!" cried the rabbit. "I am afraid to go closer!"

The lion let the little rabbit jump off his back and walked fearlessly up to the foot of the mango tree. A huge mango had fallen from the branches above and was lying there, right in front of the tree.

"Poor little rabbit," said the lion. "A mango fell to the ground and frightened you. The earth is not breaking apart. Let us go quickly and tell the other animals."

"There is no need to be afraid, dear friends," the lion said to the animals. "It was the sound of a falling mango that scared the rabbit. Sometimes we are afraid for no good reason, but blind fear can make us run toward great danger. Listen to my advice: Never believe a rumor until you have verified that it is true. Always first consider the cause of your fear, then act wisely to help yourself and others.

The little white rabbit and all the other animals promised to remember the lion's advice. Then they all returned safely to their homes in the forest.

My page

Colored by_____

The Jataka Tales nurture in readers young and old an appreciation for values shared by all the world's great traditions. Read aloud, performed and studied for centuries, they communicate universal values such as kindness, forgiveness, compassion, humility, courage, honesty and patience. You can bring these stories alive through the suggestions on these pages. Actively engaging with the stories creates a bridge to the children in your life and opens a dialogue about what brings joy, stability and caring.

The Rabbit Who Overcame Fear

A little white rabbit taking a nap is startled awake by a loud noise and the ground shaking. He believes the earth is breaking apart, and scurries off in a panic. As he runs, he spreads fear among the other animals, and they nearly follow him over the edge of a cliff. A brave lion halts their flight. By asking careful questions the lion traces the "danger" back to nothing more than a fallen mango. Through his systematic exploration, the lion teaches the animals how to cope more wisely with fear.

Key Values
Coping with fear
Clear communication
Carefully examining
circumstances

Bringing the story to life

Engage the children by saying: "This tale is about a little rabbit who is afraid and inspires all the other animals to run. What might happen next?" Ask what they think will happen next each time you turn a page.

- Why was the rabbit afraid? Was he right to run away?
- What were the animals that followed him?
- How was the lion different?
- Have you ever been afraid, and why? What happened?
- When you talk to people, do you sometimes feel misunderstood, even though you thought you had spoken clearly?

Discussion topics and questions can be modified depending on the age of your child.

Teaching values through play

Follow up on the storytelling with activities that explore characters and values, and appeal to the five senses.

- Have the children color in or draw a scene or character that intrigues them. Then invite them to talk about what it means to them, exploring the key values.
- Construct and decorate masks for each character. Then have the children act out different parts of the story, playing the little white rabbit, the lion, etcetera. Have the children make a symbol for each character such as a little white tail for the rabbit, and have them hold up the symbol to speak in the voice of the character.
- Bring up a difficult or challenging situation in the child's current life; using the drawings, masks and symbols, ask the child questions such as: "What would the lion do?" "What help would the little white rabbit need, and where would he get it?"
- Have the children retell the story in their own words. Ask them to explain what motivates the animals to run away, and what the lion is trying to say.
- Make up your own story about overcoming fear. Ask the children how they would handle a similar situation. Ask them to give the story a different ending.

Active reading

- Even before children can read, they enjoy storybooks and love growing familiar with the characters and drawings. You can show them the pictures in this book and tell the story in your own words.
- By reading the book to the children two or three times and helping them to recognize words, you help them to build vocabulary.
- Children like to hear the same story over and over, with distinctive voices for all the animals.

Ganges River

INDIA

- Integrate the wisdom of the story into everyday life. When something comes up that gives rise to rumors and assumptions, remind the child how easily the little white rabbit got confused.
- Carry a book whenever you leave the house in case there is some extra time for reading.
- Talk about the story with your child while you are engaged in daily activities like washing the dishes or driving to school. Ask: "Would the lion let you hop on his back now, as you are late for school?"
- Display the key values on the refrigerator or a bulletin board — at child's eye level — and refer to them in your daily interactions.

Names and places

India: Country in Asia; the source of many spiritual traditions and the background of most of the Jataka tales. The Jatakas clarify the workings of karma and illustrate the relationship between actions and results.

Mango: A sweet and juicy fruit that can be quite large. The mango tree is indigenous to the Indian subcontinent.

We are grateful for the opportunity to offer these Jataka tales to you. May they inspire fresh insight into the dynamics of human relationships and may understanding grow with each reading.

These adaptations of Jataka tales are for children aged three to eight

JATAKA TALES SERIES